How to Be a successful Entrepreneur

Ryan M Green

Table of contents

Introduction

Who is an entrepreneur?
An entrepreneur is someone who produces, launches, and begins a new company, generally in response to an unsatisfied market demand. While specific definitions might change, often entrepreneurs are imaginative self-starters who develop full-time, successful, and sustainable firms.

Entrepreneurship might often demand big upfront investments and an early financial risk. Because of this, it might be useful for entrepreneurs to exhibit attributes like endurance, tenacity, and inventiveness that can assist their travels.

Chapter 1

Types of Entrepreneurship
Though entrepreneurship is the general process of establishing, launching, and sustaining a firm, there are many distinct forms of entrepreneurship. People have varied objectives and ideas for the sort of company they wish to develop. Everyone conducts their company based on their unique personality, abilities, and traits. Some individuals assume that through hard effort they may obtain success, while others may utilize the cash to assist them to get there. For some businesses, revenues are less essential than producing a social benefit.

Though every sort of entrepreneur confronts comparable obstacles, they may choose to approach them differently. Each kind of entrepreneur views obstacles uniquely and has distinct resources to tackle them.

Here are the many forms of entrepreneurship:

Small business entrepreneurship
Large company entrepreneurship
Scalable startup entrepreneurship
Social entrepreneurship
Innovative entrepreneurship
Hustler entrepreneurship
Imitator entrepreneurship
Researcher entrepreneurship
Buyer entrepreneurship

- **Small business entrepreneurship**
A majority of firms are small enterprises. People engaged in small company entrepreneurship are more likely to produce a profit that supports their family and a modest lifestyle. They aren't pursuing large-scale earnings or venture capital financing. Small business entrepreneurship is generally when a person owns and operates their firm. They often recruit local staff and family members. Local grocery

shops, hairdressers, tiny boutiques, consultants, and plumbers are a part of this area of entrepreneurship.

- Large company entrepreneurship
Large company entrepreneurship occurs when a firm has a limited quantity of life cycles. This form of entrepreneurship is for an accomplished expert who understands how to maintain innovation. They are generally a member of a huge team of C-level executives. Large corporations typically produce new services and products based on client preferences to suit market demand. Small business entrepreneurship may transform into huge company entrepreneurship as the firm quickly expands. This may also happen when a huge firm purchases them. Companies such as Microsoft, Google, and Disney are examples of this style of entrepreneurship.

- Scalable startup entrepreneurship

This form of entrepreneurship is when entrepreneurs think that their firm can alter the world. They typically obtain investment from venture investors and recruit specialist workers. Scalable companies seek things that are lacking in the market and build solutions for them. Many of these sorts of enterprises originate in Silicon Valley and are technology-focused. They desire quick growth and high financial returns. Examples of scalable companies include Facebook, Instagram, and Uber.

- Social entrepreneurship

An entrepreneur that aspires to tackle social issues with their goods and services is in this category of entrepreneurship. Their major purpose is to make the world a better place. They don't labor to generate enormous profits or money. Instead, these sorts of entrepreneurs choose to form NGOs or enterprises that commit themselves to work toward social good.

- Innovative entrepreneurship

Innovative entrepreneurs are people who are always coming up with fresh ideas and technologies. They take these concepts and develop them into commercial operations. They typically try to improve the way people live for the better. Innovators tend to be incredibly driven and enthusiastic individuals. They seek methods to make their goods and services stand out from other items on the market. People like Steve Jobs and Bill Gates are examples of inventive entrepreneurs.

- Hustler entrepreneurship

People that are willing to work hard and put forth consistent effort are dubbed hustler entrepreneurs. They frequently start small and strive toward establishing a larger company with hard labor rather than cash. Their objectives are what propels them, and they are prepared to do what it takes to attain their goals. They do not give up lightly and are eager to undergo hardships to accomplish what they desire. For example, someone who is a hustler is ready to cold contact several individuals to make one sale.

- Imitator entrepreneurship

Imitators are entrepreneurs that utilize others' business ideas as inspiration yet try to enhance them. They seek to make particular goods and services better and more lucrative. An imitator is a blend between an innovator and a hustler. They are prepared to think of fresh ideas and work hard, although they start by mimicking others. People who are mimics have a lot of self-confidence and drive. They may learn from others' errors while building their own company.

- Researcher entrepreneurship

Researchers take their time while launching their firms. They aim to perform as much research as possible before presenting a product or service. They feel that with the correct preparation and knowledge, they have a greater chance of being successful. Researchers make sure they grasp every area of their company and have an in-depth awareness of what they are doing. They prefer to depend on facts, evidence, and reasoning rather than their instincts. Detailed business strategies are vital to them and limit their risks of failure.

- Buyer entrepreneurship

A buyer is a sort of entrepreneur that utilizes their riches to drive their company endeavors. Their skill is to utilize their money to purchase firms that they believe will be profitable. They find potential firms and attempt to purchase them. Then, they make whatever managerial or structural adjustments they believe are required. Their objective is to develop the firms they purchase and boost their earnings. This sort of entrepreneurship is less hazardous since they are acquiring previously well-established enterprises.

Chapter 2

How To Become an Entrepreneur in 7 Steps

"Entrepreneur" is an intriguing term for many since it can be a meaningful and successful job. The entrepreneurial route tends to start with a brilliant concept. You may turn to your buddy and remark "wouldn't it be amazing if...?" Then your wheels start moving on what resources and technologies you could need to bring this vision to reality. Those interested should design a strategy and incorporate the following stages of becoming an entrepreneur:

Identify an issue.
Expand your formal and informal education.
Build your network.
Reach financial stability.
Solve the issue with a business concept.
Test the concept.
Raise money.

1. Identify an issue
After you've come up with your excellent idea—like a restaurant concept, delivery service, coaching specialty, or new app—you can next start writing the business plan. Often, you've uncovered a notion or procedure that will make consumers' lives simpler. For example, after viewing the news, an entrepreneur realizes that their city lacks appropriate childcare facilities for the working population. Through more inquiry, the entrepreneur realizes that adjacent counties suffer the same issue.

2. Expand your formal and informal education
Education is vital in an entrepreneurial career. This may be a college degree program, apprenticeship, or a variety of job experience. You will want to master the foundations of business and develop your vocabulary, as well as have excellent business acumen. Problems arise regularly

while beginning a company and understanding how to overcome them is crucial for the organization to prosper.

Before getting started, you may wish to investigate a range of success stories—and even failures—of particular company owners. Doing so, will likely both assist you to grasp the necessary persistence and encourage you to make the impossible, achievable. Start by following businesses from your institution or alma mater or even identify influencers on social networking sites. Famous entrepreneurs who have had a demonstrable influence with their initiatives include Oprah Winfrey, Steve Jobs, Richard Branson, Marc Cuban, Anne Wojcicki, Reshma Saujani, Sara Blakely, Kendra Scott, Bill Gates, and Michael Dell.

3. Build your network
It might be tough to get a business endeavor going, but you can make it simpler by soliciting support from other experts or

mentors. Those that take the effort to network and develop new relationships might reap tremendous rewards. Contacts may give useful beginning loans, pertinent advice, or provide new and better chances.

Look for entrepreneurs among family, friends, neighbors, or university alumni networks and reach out to them for informational interviews. Consider yourself an investigative reporter and make it your aim to learn two to three things from each of them about entrepreneurship. Take extensive notes.

Also, take the time to study angel investors and financing for entrepreneurs and small business grants.

4. Reach financial stability
Although it's feasible to receive more financing, experts suggest that young entrepreneurs have a significant amount of savings, because they may lose money on

their first venture. Do not hesitate to engage with a financial professional on what your P&L (Profits & Losses) spreadsheet may look like one, two, and three years away. Many entrepreneurs discover that they truly start to earn a profit in three to five years and a lot may happen in the market during that period. If you have a backup source of income, support, or an extra pool of money, this may make the transition to a new company concept simpler to handle and assist in educating your expectations.

5. Solve the issue with a business concept Continuing with the previous scenario, the entrepreneur's idea is to create a daycare center with numerous business partners that support the tri-county region. With so many firms employing parents with little children and no company presently offering stable daycare, there are enough clients and cash to be generated. Entrepreneur may now create their company strategy.

6. Test the concept
The entrepreneur's concept is strong, but
they need to test it. Local business owners
are the greatest place to start. So, the
entrepreneur surveys various company
owners in the region, gauging their
demand—and the need of others they may
know—for daycare. Results demonstrate
that the great majority are unhappy with
their existing childcare, citing lengthy
commutes and/or job disruption as their top
concerns.

The entrepreneur learns two crucial pieces
of information:

Most community members require the
service.
There are three significant companies with a
sufficient volume of workers and possible
onsite childcare space.
A competition analysis might reveal areas of
improvement in the company strategy.

7. Raise money
It's nice to have money to fall back on, but
the entrepreneur may need a lot more to
start the firm. There are three major
methods to get capital:

Bootstrap. This word refers to the act of
beginning a company without support. It
may be done by decreasing expenses or
utilizing an individual's own money.
Apply for a loan. A frequent approach for
acquiring funds is applying for a bank loan.
It may not be feasible to apply for a small
company loan thus early on. However,
people may apply for general loans to cover
start-up expenditures.

Find an investor. Networking assists in
discovering people who can give financial
assistance. Pitching a company concept to
an angel investor is a terrific alternative.
Otherwise, the person may need to
approach a venture capitalist business.
These companies need entrepreneurs and

their enterprises to satisfy particular standards to apply.

Chapter 3

Frequently asked questions about becoming an entrepreneur

If you're considering becoming an entrepreneur, you certainly have numerous questions. Here are the most typical questions you could have:

- Are there any educational requirements?
- How can young entrepreneurs market their firms on their own?
- Do entrepreneurs need to be creative?
- How can novice entrepreneurs establish a firm on their own?
- What are the typical challenges to starting an entrepreneur?
- Can you start a company in college?

1. Are there any educational requirements?

Entrepreneurs are in business for themselves. Since they're generally their employer, entrepreneurs may not require a college education. There are many useful tools on the internet to aid folks on their new professional routes. Having a college degree might be quite advantageous, though. degrees in business, economics, or a similar discipline give excellent insight into the profession. Earning a Master's in Business Administration may appear better to prospective investors than having no degree at all.

A lot of life experience might also assist. For example, if you have worked in customer service, hospitality, the service sector, or even healthcare, you have a genuine feel of many factors to make a firm effective and also unanticipated events. This might allow you to be adaptive and flexible to mix your learning with your action steps to bring your concept to life.

2. How can young entrepreneurs market their firms on their own?

Advertising is costly and demands good teaching to comprehend. For people without degrees, the internet offers information and even basic courses for advertising. Entrepreneurs may not always require a complex marketing or scripted ad. They may instead employ digital marketing to publicize their firm. Social media networks enable company owners to advertise on their sites and even give guidelines on how to utilize their ad management systems.

One crucial factor is to consider the impact of "word-of-mouth" marketing. You may wish to understand your target market and how they would assist to be your greatest advocate. This involves being clear about your beliefs, purpose, goods, and services as well as how you're distinct from your competitors.

3. Do entrepreneurs need to be creative?

It is useful to harness creativity to design a
company as the entrepreneur's purpose is to
come up with innovative solutions to issues.
Each entrepreneur may have a distinct sense
of creativity (art, marketing, financing,
promotions, partners) (art, marketing,
finances, promotions, partners). It is crucial
to have strong abilities such as mathematics
and problem-solving to fully bring your
ideas to life.

If you prefer to exercise your creative brain,
here are two sites to try:

Design thinking
Knowing your strengths

4. How can novice entrepreneurs
   establish a firm on their own?
To establish a firm, entrepreneurs need to
educate themselves about the sector they're
entering. They need to grasp the needs and
expectations required for success. Financing
might be tough thus early in a young

entrepreneur's career, but they can aid the enterprise by simply investing in what is essential for the firm to run.

5. What are the typical challenges to starting an entrepreneur?

One of the greatest challenges is just coming up with a decent concept. Many aspects influence a company's concept such as location, audience, and general need. Many novice entrepreneurs just perceive their concept at face value, not recognizing that these aspects may be important to its success. Another significant hurdle is the lack of opportunity. If someone desire to create a company in a certain town or city, they should investigate the region to make sure there is a demand for their product or service. There are many unknowns in business, therefore it needs someone with persistence, a desire to learn, and a passion to make their vision come to reality.

Many entrepreneurs find enormous benefits in maintaining a day job while they establish their side company. This enables them to have the resources to cover their day-to-day obligations and commit their passion to their side project—although it might seem like it may take longer that way. Some may say that this doesn't enable you to commit yourself but it may alleviate the first financial strain so that you don't burn out too early.

Another crucial ability that cannot be disregarded is to network, network, network. You will need several areas of support for your new firm to flourish so be sure to arrange a time to talk with possible partners, investors, customers, sales, or technology specialists. You may start by joining networking organizations in your region.

Some examples—and you may discover ones that are a fit for your talents and interests:

Affiliate organizations: Black Accountants
Talent Network
National professional organizations:
American Marketing Association
Women's groups: Herdacity, Prowess
Project, and Forte Foundation
Industry groups: Search LinkedIn or
Meetup for areas of interest
Pro Tip: You can even establish your own
with another enterprising pal. Use this as an
opportunity to invite speakers and give a
range of entrepreneurial courses within your
community.

6. Can you start a company in college?
You may become an entrepreneur in college,
but it needs a strong belief and drive to
succeed. Students need to commit time and
focus to both their academics and their
business and maintain a good balance. If
you decide to start a company while still in
college, consider how issues like student

loans may affect your credit or the amount of money you will need to earn.

Explore resources and networking organizations on campus so you have the support of individuals who may be pursuing their business ideas. This will also enable you to meet and greet local businesses, engage in pitch competitions, and be exposed to many who may assist disseminate your concept and present you to wonderful partners and areas of consideration to work toward success.

Chapter 4

Entrepreneur Characteristics To Develop for Success

Entrepreneur attributes are qualities that help entrepreneurs accomplish their aims. An entrepreneur is someone who establishes, organizes, and operates a firm. Examples of entrepreneurs include:

Online business owners: Online entrepreneurs include bloggers, e-commerce, or any company owner who undertakes commercial activity largely online.

Home-based company owners: A house-based entrepreneur conducts their business from their home, as opposed to an office.

Inventors: Inventors are entrepreneurs who create their concept and sell it on the market.

Small business owners: Small enterprises employ fewer than 500 people.

In every situation, entrepreneurship includes inventing new ideas, putting them into action, and persisting through hurdles. Some entrepreneur qualities are innate personality traits, but there are other abilities and attributes you may build through practice.

Here are 15 attributes you may develop to become a successful entrepreneur:
1. Creativity
2. Passion
3. Motivation
4. Product or service knowledge
5. Ability to network
6. Self-confidence
7. Optimism
8. Vision
9. Goal mindset
10. Risk-taking
11. Persuasiveness
12. Decision-making
13. Tenacity
14. Money management

15.Adaptability

1. Creativity

Becoming an entrepreneur begins with an idea. You need to recognize possibilities, discover unique ways to accomplish things, and deliver answers to the public.

To boost your creativity, create behaviors that promote the creative system. Think about what helps you feel creative, such as music, meeting people, reading, or any other activity. Dedicate a certain section of your day to discovering inspiration for fresh ideas. During this time of the day, start by doing what inspires you, then let your thoughts flow. You may construct a list of ideas and pick those to pursue.

2. Passion

Passion is what drives entrepreneurs. They typically enjoy what they do, and this helps them spend their time on their initiatives.

To become a more passionate entrepreneur, concentrate on the significance of your job. Remember that you contribute to developing answers that will assist many others. Knowing that your devotion has an effect may give you the energy you need to continue when uncertainty comes in or when the business gets challenging. Passion is what keeps you focused on your aim.

3. Motivation
Motivation is the will to do particular objectives. Entrepreneurs are determined to make their firm a success and push themselves.

To enhance motivation, you might start by creating minor objectives. Small objectives may help you attain bigger ones and push you to seek higher. Recognize the job previously performed and enjoy your successes, even modest ones. Also, have a cheerful outlook. Turn your thoughts away from negativity and everyday hurdles to concentrate on what you want to accomplish and the good parts of your life.

4. Product or service knowledge
Entrepreneurs know what they have to give and to whom they can sell it. Identify the type of items or services you offer and how they bring value to customers. Also, investigate your target clientele to make sure you satisfy their wants. This will help you to upgrade your offer continually so you can keep on top of industry trends.

To boost the beneficial effect of this information, you should consistently learn about your market, understand what customers need, and know the aspects that separate you from rivals. Talk with your clientele and utilize their input. With this information, you may modify your posture as required.

5. Ability to network

The capacity to connect with people and to spot chances for cooperation is important to a successful business. Meeting new individuals could allow access to resources or information that your firm requires. It helps you to learn from the success of others, market your services or products and meet new clientele.

To increase your networking abilities, you must aim to develop real contacts. You undoubtedly have a corporate aim in mind, but approach individuals with the intention of a personal connection, just like meeting new friends. If you meet someone who might benefit another person in your network, link them. Not only will you assist someone, but they will probably remember you and wish to return the favor.

6. Self-confidence
Entrepreneurs feel they can accomplish their aims. They may have reservations, but they persist through them. They are eager to

engage in the required effort because they are certain they can develop something greater than what now exists.

Self-confidence is crucial since it helps you to feel better and makes it easier to overcome problems, take chances and be persistent. Therefore, it adds to your success overall.

To boost your self-confidence, you might employ the practice of visualization. Envision yourself as the person you want to be and visualize your company at a level you would be proud of. You may also practice affirmation by speaking encouraging words about your successes. These approaches may assist to improve the way you perceive yourself favorably.

7. Optimism
Entrepreneurs are visionaries with a strategy in place: They see the good side of the situation and constantly move ahead.

Optimism fosters creativity, thus it helps business leaders uncover new ideas for their goods or services and boosts their chances of success.

To improve your optimism, you might regard setbacks as chances to progress instead of issues that could stop you. Keep the eventual objective in mind, and don't linger on previous difficulties.

8. Vision
Entrepreneurs have a vision. They envision a broad picture they aspire to complete, which feeds their efforts and motivates them to do more. Moreover, vision is what establishes the culture and identity of a business. Not only does it keep entrepreneurs enthusiastic, but it helps them to encourage others and keep them working towards the company's success.

To strengthen your entrepreneurial vision, you may create a daily action plan.

Prioritizing your work might save you from feeling overwhelmed and help you stick to your goal. Also, listen to or read inspiring information to reinforce your mind and keep focused on your objective.

9. Goal mindset
Entrepreneurs are goal-oriented. They know what they want to accomplish, establish a goal and strive toward that target. Determination is crucial to conquering probable hurdles, and it also inspires trust from the individuals who work with you.

To become more goal-oriented, you may start by establishing what you want to achieve and articulating your vision of the future. Then, define a goal with a deadline to direct your efforts. This will enable you to watch your growth and help keep you devoted to your objective.

10. Risk-taking
Entrepreneurs are willing to take risks. They prepare for the unknown so they can make calculated judgments that are advantageous for them and their company.

To boost your risk-taking skills, you might start treating your trip as a learning experience, including the probable failures. You must keep your objective in mind and commit to enduring.

It is vital to take certain chances to separate from your competitors and enable your firm to flourish. Once you realize how you can handle risk and develop from setbacks, you may feel more comfortable with pushing yourself.

11. Persuasiveness
Entrepreneurs know their company and how to communicate about it to others. They need to convince people to believe in their notion.

To increase your persuasive abilities, learn about your listeners and adapt to their personalities. You may offer a tale to engage them on an emotional level and convey your devotion. If people can relate to your narrative, it establishes a connection that may blossom into loyalty, which is vital for your business's success. Another approach is to discuss your successes and depend on facts to back your claims and persuade others.

12. Decision-making
Entrepreneurs need to make rapid judgments and take action for the success of their firm.

To strengthen your decision-making abilities, you may enlighten yourself to comprehend better the challenges you strive to address. Assess the effect of the choice you need to make, and allocate a proportional amount of time to deliberate.

You may also filter your selections to facilitate the process of choosing a decision.

13. Tenacity
Entrepreneurs overcome hurdles. They endure despite adversities and hang on to their ambitions and aspirations.

To strengthen your tenacity, you might write down your objectives and read them every day. You may pick role models and recall famous characters of history who had to endure failure before they attained achievement.

14. Money management
Entrepreneurs need to comprehend the financial position of their firm. Even if they engage an expert like an accountant, they are the decision-maker and must comprehend their position to operate the firm effectively.

You may enhance your fundamental money management abilities by making a budget and adhering to it and investing available dollars rather than wasting them. You may also learn additional financial information by completing courses or training programs.

15. Adaptability
When they start a company, entrepreneurs typically need to multitask. Flexibility in your schedule, as well as in your thoughts, is vital to continue learning in hard conditions.

To develop your flexibility, you may approach all activities with an open mind and be ready to adjust your approaches if required. Try new ways and accept new trends to encourage your capacity to adapt.

Chapter 5

Entrepreneurial Traits To Develop for Career Success

Entrepreneurial attributes are the usual features, talents, and thinking processes associated with successful entrepreneurs. While some entrepreneurs are born with certain abilities, others may develop them. These include:

1. Being a good leader

An entrepreneur is supposed to run a company and most people in this position are responsible for its start-up as well. Typically, entrepreneurship requires identifying and creating partnerships with investors, controlling staff, and monitoring operations. To accomplish these duties, you need to be an effective leader.

Leadership is the capacity to lead others. A successful leader mobilizes people to accomplish objectives and is viewed as a leader by their followers. There are methods in which you may foster this feature, such as:

Learning from your experiences
As it is common to make errors while managing a team, you may analyze the positives and negatives of your leadership style while you work and utilize your discoveries to enhance how you lead others.

Researching the various leadership styles
For example, the democratic style of leadership, which includes greater cooperation between leaders and followers in the process of decision-making, may be useful during the first stage of building up a firm. It may provide a company superior insights for decision-making when recruiting a huge team of specialists is not practical.

Learning about the top in your business

You may discover how industry leaders manage their main stakeholders and adopt the leadership approaches that work for your organization.

Developing an approach to leadership that works for you
By examining various types of leadership and reviewing your leadership style, you might discover a leadership style that matches you and your organization.

2. Being hopeful

Optimism may be characterized as concentrating on the positives and being emotionally resilient to problems. An entrepreneur who organizes manages and executes a firm is likely to experience several setbacks over time. For example, if you start your firm, you will need to fill out a lot of paperwork covering permits, tax forms, business plans, and bank accounts. In the course of having these papers ready, there might be numerous obstacles that check your progress, such as delays in receiving a license or structural flaws in your company plan.

Being positive might allow you to solve these challenges quickly instead of feeling demotivated by them. Like the other crucial entrepreneurial attributes, optimism is a skill that you will need to acquire and retain throughout your profession. There are methods in which you may foster optimism, such as:

Surrounding oneself with positivity by employing positive personnel, putting inspiring quotations in your interior design, or listening to uplifting music
Developing an optimistic view that affects the way you conduct things in your organization and affects your decision-making process
Starting to look at regular happenings as business possibilities

Identifying the advantages in a troublesome situation and concentrating on them as you troubleshoot
Finding a job coach who can enable you to build your optimism
Catching yourself being pessimistic and altering your perspective. For example, you might start looking at challenges that check your development as learning experiences that can prepare you for greater success in the future.

3. Being confident
Confidence is a subjective perception that you have what is required for anything. Entrepreneurs seek banks for loans, employ workers, encourage teams, and establish connections with customers and suppliers, thus an entrepreneur must be confident in their abilities to do all these things successfully.

Being confident may improve your company. Key stakeholders are more likely to react positively to your offers if you express your confidence. You may utilize numerous strategies to become more confident, such as:

Cultivate a conviction in yourself and your talents. Make a note of your triumphs and remind yourself of them in times of uncertainty. For example, tell yourself that you are creating something that people want to purchase or remind yourself of the things that you have already done to make your company more successful.
Plan and do your everyday tasks with the idea that you will accomplish them even if there are difficulties.
Research how confidence may be transmitted via nonverbal and vocal communication and apply these tactics to enhance how you present yourself.
Role-play scenarios like talks with major suppliers or conversations with investors by practicing your message delivery, learning

to answer common questions, and managing criticism effectively.

Hire a professional coach who can assist you to increase your confidence.

Spend time with people who have a good influence on the way that you feel about yourself. These social events may boost your confidence.

Learn new hard and soft skills to boost your job performance. This will help you become more self-assured at work.

Make improvements that may enhance your look such as dressing nicely, exercising frequently, and eating healthily to raise your confidence.

4. Being passionate

Being enthusiastic about establishing and operating your company might make it simpler to put in the work required for a successful organization. If you need to enhance your work enthusiasm, try these tips:

Try to conceive of your profession as more than simply a living and create a real passion for what you do. You may remind yourself of why you chose to establish your own company or think about the good benefits that your business has on yourself, your staff, your customers, or your community.

Start each work day by reminding yourself of all the things that you look forward to accomplishing such as completing a sale or recruiting a new employee.

Learn how to convey your enthusiasm whether you deal with workers, suppliers, or investors. Your excitement for what you do might make your primary stakeholders feel more enthused too, which could assist your firm.

5. Being disciplined

Being disciplined may enable you to attain success as an entrepreneur. Entrepreneurs are expected to work individually, establish their objectives and overcome difficulties. To execute these tasks properly, being disciplined is vital. You may utilize the following suggestions to become more disciplined:

Train yourself to be a self-starter who begins and completes work without the need for scrutiny.
Give yourself a tiny reward each time you fulfill a goal. This will inspire you to attain your objectives without being sidetracked.
Develop a work ethic that motivates your resolve to work hard to attain your professional objectives. Keep in mind that many entrepreneurs who have founded successful firms have spent more time at work than most of their workers.
6. Being proactive
A proactive person anticipates possibilities and dangers and seeks to handle them whereas a reactive person merely responds to them. As an entrepreneur, it is always preferable to be proactive than of being reactive. Here are some ways in which you might become more proactive:

Combine research with active listening to understand the demands of important stakeholders (your customers, employers, and business partners) (your customers, employers, and business partners).
Identify dangers in events and seek remedies before these concerns become more serious.
Analyze your business activities periodically. Identify the areas that may be improved and enhance these aspects.
Try to build long-term solutions to address the primary causes of difficulties instead of producing short-term fixes that are unsuccessful.
Use verbal and written communication to show staff that you accept their comments. This can assist you to discover areas that need to be improved or policies that need to be communicated more clearly to staff.

7. Keeping an open mind
Keeping an open mind entails the openness to listen to the thoughts and ideas of others. Typically, entrepreneurs start enterprises in competitive sectors that have previously established market leaders. To thrive in this job, it is vital to find business possibilities in daily occurrences and seek methods to increase company offers. Consider the following strategies to cultivate this trait:

Be ready to listen to others instead of refusing to realize that someone else possibly has a worthwhile perspective. This might boost your reservoir of thoughts and insights.

Encourage employees or consumers to submit feedback and consider their thoughts to make a product or service better.

Use fresh ideas or insights about processes, customer service, or staff involvement to enhance a product or service offering.

8. Being competitive

Competitiveness is an important quality among successful businesses. With globalization and virtualization, industries become more competitive. To sustain a prosperous firm, it is vital to cultivate a competitive mindset. Consider the following tips to improve your competitiveness:

Keep track of what your rivals are doing using market research and market-monitoring services, and ensure that you do not fall behind in terms of development.

Identify the business methods that work for your rivals as well as the ones that do not work, and employ these tactics to better your firm.

Use product innovations, price, marketing, and distribution to make your items more competitive in the market. For example, you may price a new product in a market with numerous existing brands at a relatively cheap price and spend on innovative advertising to convince buyers to switch brands and try your product.

Develop consumer analytics and utilize your results to maintain enhancing your goods or services by making them more adaptable to client wants.

Use employee studies to build incentives like perks, severance packages, and performance-based prizes to recruit the finest employees to your team.

9. Being nice

While compassion is not typically considered a vital attribute among businesses, it might aid you in retaining success. For example, although it is simple to concentrate on fulfilling your KPIs on sales, neglecting to consider the well-being of your staff or disregarding the influence that a manufacturing process has on your community might cause you issues over time or enable your rivals to gain an edge.

You may utilize the following strategies to build kindness:

Assess the working circumstances of your full-time workers often and ensure that they have the fundamentals they need to function properly.
Re-evaluate your employee benefits frequently to make sure that you are delivering a package that can support employees as well as attract top people.
Be proactive in upgrading your production or distribution operations to make them less detrimental to the environment and more sustainable.
Foster a friendly, healthy business culture with solid regulations that prohibit bullying, sexual harassment, or gender-based discrimination.

Chapter 6

When (and How) to Say "No" To Opportunities

To obtain some perspective on how I may better analyze my choices and be pickier when analyzing the chances that would truly benefit me, I asked some of the ultra-successful guests on my podcast about how they go about making decisions.

Here's the advice that I've found most useful.

- Outsmart the pleasure principle.
One of the pitfalls I fall into is saying yes to an opportunity merely because it is in the far future, at a period when my calendar is blissfully vacant, and clearing out my planner makes me feel more productive. I say to myself, Sure, it seems enjoyable, and it looks like I have time for it.

Saying yes is also simpler than saying no. It takes less time and needs no careful explanation. But, when the event ultimately comes around, I start to regret my choice, as my schedule has gotten unmanageable.

Sigmund Freud famously referred to these short-term benefits for long-term suffering as the pleasure principle, our predisposition as humans to seek pleasure and avoid pain. When we promptly answer yes, we are welcomed with a favorable reaction from the requester, which makes us feel good – particularly if we have a practice of pleasing people. However, the pain comes up further down the road, when we have to follow through.

One of the guests on my show, a motivational guru, Turia Pitt, told me that she used to find herself constantly slipping into this trap. Pitt is regularly invited to deliver talks many months in advance. "I say to myself, 'Oh, it's like in six months, whatever, it'll be fine,'" she added. "And then when the speech is looming, I'll be like, 'Oh my god, why did I say yes?'"

To interrupt the loop, Pitt started to take ask herself three questions before answering demands for her time: If this opportunity or event was occurring next Tuesday, how would I feel about it? Would I be like, "Yes! I cannot wait for it to happen"? Or would I be fearing it?

If she doesn't feel especially thrilled about whatever opportunity is being provided, then her response is plain.

I now ask myself this question, and I find it helps me hone in on how I feel about any possibility I'm exploring. If you too struggle with saying no, it's a tactic I advocate.

- Estimate the time (generously) (generously).

Another difficulty I have regularly run across is greatly underestimating the time required. In fact, I do say yes. For example, a few years ago, I was requested to sit on a committee to examine the MBA program of a famous Australian business school.

I have some strong ideas on how MBA programs may best prepare graduates for leadership jobs, and given that my consulting business had hired numerous MBA students from this university in the past, I was selfishly driven to brainstorm how it might create even more successful graduates. So, as usual, I consented.

After my first rigorous three-hour meeting, I instantly regretted my choice.

Ex-Google initiatives designer and author, John Zeratsky, refers to my dilemma as the "Iceberg Yes." "When we are selecting whether to pursue anything — a project, a job, a volunteer position, and so on — we tend to concentrate on the visible and exciting component. In other words, we concentrate on the shimmering pinnacle of the iceberg that stands above the water." Zeratsky reminds out that the bulk of the time commitment remains concealed below the surface.

When Zeratsky gets requests for his time, he thinks about the full iceberg — not just what is above the surface. He analyzes all the labor that will be necessary before getting to the fun aspects. He also evaluates how much time it will take out of his usual job routine.

"For example, when I accept a speaking job, I also arrange the time to prepare for that performance. It makes it tougher to say yes, but that's a good thing."

I find the Iceberg Yes technique especially handy when determining whether to say yes to audio guest pitches. In addition to completing the actual interview, I question myself, "Would I feel eager to spend four to eight hours studying this individual in preparation for the interview?" The answer to this question makes my selection straightforward.

The next time you are asked to do something that initially looks exciting — such as writing a guest blog post, sitting on a panel, or speaking on a subject that you're passionate about - pause and think about how much less interesting work will be involved if you say yes.

Is the entire time commitment something you can fit into your schedule? If it is, you consider saying yes with confidence, knowing you will be able to provide.

- Adopt some harsh regulations.

Finally, the act of making choices demands a lot of energy. Research on decision fatigue reveals that the more choices we make over a day, the poorer our decision-making gets owing to limited willpower reserves. As such, I have found success in establishing hard and fast guidelines for myself to assist shorten the decision-making process.

I frame my regulations with the phrase "I don't..." (I don't do X; I don't do Y) to make it seem like the rule is a legitimate part of my personality.

I have a rule, for instance, that I don't talk at dinner gatherings. I've had some ordinary experiences making keynote speeches to rooms full of inebriated people and it's not something that I intend to do again in this lifetime. Instead of having to deliberately analyze every possibility that takes happen during a dinner event or cocktail hour, I just remark to the organizer, "I don't talk at dinner events."

When designing your guidelines, consider your abilities and the sort of activities that excite you. For example, you may feel incredibly uncomfortable attending networking events, yet know that creating networks is vital for your profession. For example, you can give yourself a rule that you don't attend networking events since they're not good for you, but instead, you proactively reach out to individuals for one-on-one discussions to expand your networks in a less anxiety-provoking method.

Choosing between possibilities or saying yes or no to chances is challenging — but being intentional in how you make decisions may be the difference between a successful and satisfying life, and one that is substantially less so.

Chapter 7

How to Be an Entrepreneur Who Doesn't Suck

Here's the sugar-coated version of what I'm going to say: Starting your first firm comes with a learning curve.

Now here's the harsh-but-true version: A lot of young entrepreneurs simply plain stink at being the boss.

Blunt as it sounds, it's also sensible - there's no question that entrepreneurship is hard. Having just left a position at an established business to build my first startup, a big data security analytics firm called Exabeam, I've learned a lot about how to negotiate the logistics of establishing a new company and make it operate as efficiently as possible. With that in mind, here are my five top pieces of advice for first-time entrepreneurs:

Don't strike out on your own too early. If you don't have a desire to create, you're probably not ready to be an entrepreneur. A great entrepreneur has to have a true fire in his belly, something that makes him enthusiastic about beginning something new. Without such desire, the journey is considerably difficult. As much as I liked my prior career, after 10 years I thought it was time to establish something new. If you don't feel that drive, it can be an indication that you need more time to prepare yourself emotionally and professionally.

Hire the appropriate individuals... When you've thrown your efforts into launching a firm, the urge to control and handle everything yourself is powerful. Hiring "soul players" - individuals who put their heart and soul into creating the business and solving challenges - may give you the confidence required to trust your staff and offer them the flexibility to make choices that improve the firm. Look for enthusiastic, motivated individuals with whom you're thrilled to work, and make sure they mix well with the corporate culture. Maintain that team approach and you'll establish a crew that's capable of fast-growing your business.\s...and recruit them wisely. Be modest and acknowledge that you don't know everything. Let the gaps in your expertise guide your recruiting process. Find individuals who have the abilities you need, and search for a broad spectrum of competence in your personnel. That way, everyone is allowed to play to his or her strengths, and the team's strength will make up for any individual deficiencies - yours included.

Don't be frightened of failure. No matter how brilliant, skilled, or thorough you are, you will fail at some point throughout the process of starting a firm. No one loves to fail, but you may utilize failure to continue learning and improving. Take the losses in stride, and train yourself to recover gracefully and learn from your errors. This is the nature of the beast when it comes to taking chances, and without them, you won't have much success. Be courageous when it comes to developing and growing since such chances will ultimately pay off.

Keep learning. Even if you're an expert in your profession, establishing a firm sends you back to square one in many respects. There are numerous things an entrepreneur must do that you probably never even considered in your prior employment. Use your experience to your advantage, of course, but have an open mind and continue to improve your skill set. It's also crucial to keep your ego in control. Your advisers, investors, and workers all bring significant talents and experiences to the table. Learn from them.

You will always run across obstacles while beginning your first firm. Whether it's a setback in personnel, marketing, business, or production, something will not go as you hoped it would. There's nothing you can do to avert such barriers, and that's good. With the correct mentality, a competent team, and honest analysis of your requirements, you can avoid sucking as a first-time entrepreneur.

Chapter 8

Stop These Negative Mindsets That Make Entrepreneurs Miserable

Being an entrepreneur is far from easy. Sleepless nights, continuous stress, and donning numerous hats, are usual. From the outside looking in, it could seem that it's all rainbows and sunshine, but ask even the most successful entrepreneurs whether it was simple — they will shake their heads and grin.

So, how can you maintain relatively sane during the business journey? The solution is simple: be joyful. When you love what you do, happiness isn't far behind. There are, nevertheless, certain factors that will keep you back. So, avoid doing these eight things and you will be a happy entrepreneur.

1. Seeking the approval of others.
You must learn how to trust your instincts and make choices that affect your company

on your own. It doesn't matter how fantastic and feasible your ideas may be, there will always be some who reject them if you seek permission.

We naturally want to make everyone happy, particularly when it comes to friends and family — but unless they are in the trenches with you and share the same vision, their opinion will just stress you out, leading you to make terrible business choices.

2. Pointing the blame to others.
When stuff hits the fan — and ultimately it will — it's extremely simple to blame someone or something else. As an entrepreneur, you are ultimately accountable for everything that occurs inside your firm. Even if an employee royally messes up, you are liable. You made the hiring choice, so now you must repair the holes and fix the ship before it sinks.

A fellow entrepreneur and CEO of Aucto, Jamil Rahman, once stated to me, "The sooner you own up to your error, the sooner you can take action to remedy it." This simple piece of advice may avoid a lot of unneeded headaches and worry.

3. Not believing in oneself.
What is one attribute that all great entrepreneurs have in common? They all believe in themselves — they have 100 percent faith that they can win — at anything and everything.

If you question your talents, those negative ideas will control and destroy you. Confidence and positive thinking are highly strong combos that may help you attain any goal you set. "Whatever the mind can imagine and believe, it can accomplish," concluded Napoleon Hill, author of Think and Grow Rich.

4. Complaining.
Complaining will never get you anywhere.
It's simply a massive waste of time, and the
longer you moan about anything, the longer
it will take you to find a solution to cure the
problem. If you seek a stress-free
profession, entrepreneurship is not for you.

There are going to be numerous barriers in
your path that will stress you out and you
will most likely be knocked down a few
times — failure is highly feasible.
Complaining is a productivity-suck that will
royally interfere with your objectives and
concentration. Be tough and be ready for
obstacles.

5. Being terrified of change.
Change is a typical event for an
entrepreneur. A shift of corporate direction
following a pivot, a change in location, or
even a change in the industry. When you set
that fear aside and welcome change, it opens
the path to pleasure.

I'll give you a perfect example: I was active in various sectors before I launched my internet marketing consulting firm. I wasn't pleased, so I did some pondering. What I came to learn was that the one element of my business that I enjoyed was the marketing side, so I decided to abandon everything and launch Market Domination Media. Was it terrifying at first? You bet, but it ended up being a terrific move — and it wouldn't have occurred had I been terrified of change.

6. Expecting to win 100 percent of the time. Does David Ortiz walk out to bat expecting to smash a home run every time? Does Tom Brady hope to deliver a touchdown pass every offensive play? No. While they are confident in their ability, they recognize that they aren't going to smash home runs and throw TDs every time out there.

Entrepreneurs need to go into each circumstance understanding that they can't win every time. While confidence is necessary, it requires a tiny element of realism mixed in. If you expect to win every time, that first defeat will be painful and a motivation killer.

7. Giving up.
One of my favorite entrepreneurial facts is about James Dyson, designer of Dyson vacuum cleaners. If he quit, the world's most successful vacuum would have never been developed. He developed 5,127 prototypes of the vacuum, all failures before the first successful model was manufactured. It was 15 years of never letting up that today Dyson is valued at around $5 billion.

While most people in his situation would have resigned after a few failures — maybe even a dozen — he was so determined, that he pushed hard for fifteen years and more than five thousand unsuccessful prototypes. "Giving up" was not in his lexicon.

8. Trying to impress.
I'm going to make this one short and sweet: don't fall for the social media bling factor. So many individuals attempt to impress — photographs of cars, watches, mansions, holidays, etc. Sadly, the bulk of it is all false and designed to draw people in.

Instead of stressing about impressing others, spend your emphasis on these three things: your business, health, and family. That is the actual prescription for happiness.